I0762676

Little Mitchie

GAME DAY GRUB

RECIPES FOR EVERY SPORT

KIDS IN THE KITCHEN

Joanne Mattern

CREATING YOUNG NONFICTION READERS

Little Mitchie books spark curiosity and support early nonfiction reading for students in Grades 2-3. Designed to build vocabulary, support second language learners, and prepare readers for middle-grade content, each book includes helpful tips for parents and educators to build confidence and deepen understanding of the world.

TIPS FOR READING NONFICTION WITH BEGINNING READERS

Talk about Nonfiction

Begin by explaining that nonfiction books give us information that is true. The book will be organized around a specific topic or idea, and we may learn new facts through reading.

Look at the Parts

Most nonfiction books have helpful features. Our *Little Mitchie* titles include color photographs and graphic aids, a table of contents, a glossary, and an index. Share the purpose of these features with your reader.

Color Photos and Graphic Aids

A lot of information can be found by "reading" photos, charts, maps, and other graphic aids found within nonfiction texts. Help your reader learn more about the different ways information can be displayed.

Table of Contents

Located at the front of the book, this list shows the big ideas within the text and the page numbers where they can be found.

Glossary

Located at the back of the book, the glossary defines key words and phrases that are related to the topic. These words and phrases can be found in the text in colored type.

Index

Located at the back of the book, an index is an alphabetical list of topics and the page numbers where they can be found.

With a little help and guidance about reading nonfiction, you can feel good about introducing a young reader to the world of *Little Mitchie* nonfiction books.

Little Mitchie is an imprint of:

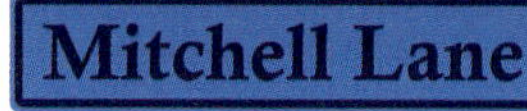

PUBLISHERS

2001 SW 31st Avenue
Hallandale, FL 33009
mitchelllanepub.com

First Edition, 2027.

Author: Joanne Mattern
Designer: Bobbie Houser
Editor: Madison Greve

Library of Congress Cataloging-in-Publication Data
Title: Game Day Grub: Recipes for Every Sport /
by Joanne Mattern

Description: Hallandale, FL :
Mitchell Lane Publishers, [2027]

Identifiers:
ISBN 979-8-89260-926-5 (library bound)
ISBN 979-8-90145-012-3 (eBook)

Library of Congress Control Number: 2026936530

PHOTO CREDITS
Shutterstock: TheCamdenStreet Design, cover, 1, 15; Taras Grebinets, 4; Viktoriia Ablohina, 5; Elena Veselova, 7; Carolyn Franks, 9; Megan Betteridge, 11; Sohel_ctg, 13; Arfin Studio, 17; nana77777, 19; Nina Buday, 21.

TABLE OF CONTENTS

HOW TO USE THIS BOOK

The kitchen is a great place to have fun! This book will help you make some delicious recipes.

Read each recipe first. Be sure to have everything you need in place before you start. Check that no one is **allergic** to any of the ingredients.

Wash your hands before you start.

Have an adult close by. Let them use knives and the stove.

Now, get ready to cook up some fun!

CONVERSION CHART

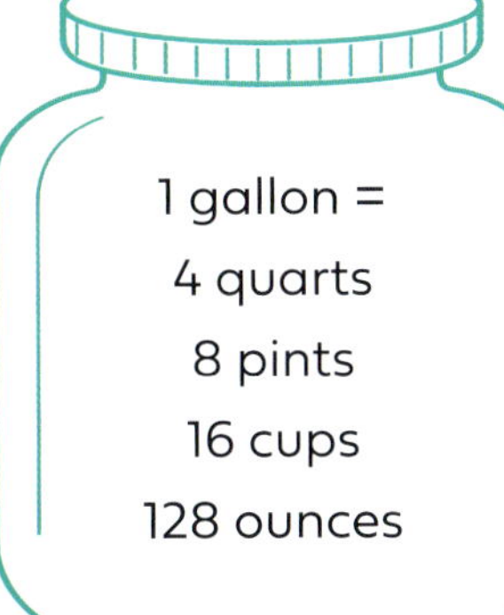

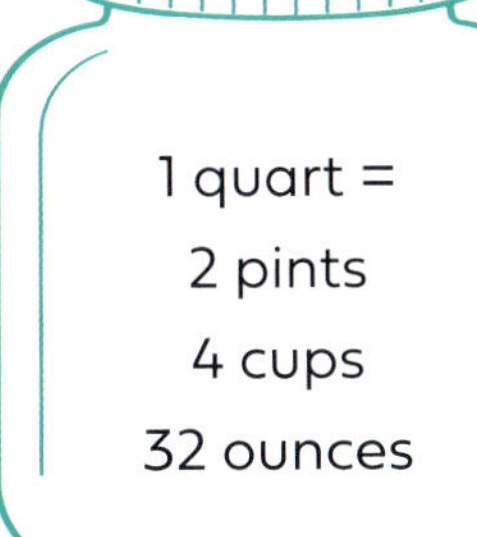

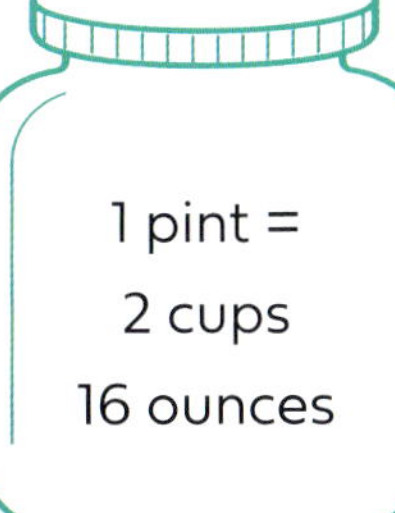

1 cup =
16 tablespoons
8 ounces

¾ cup =
12 tablespoons
6 ounces

½ cup =
8 tablespoons
4 ounces

⅓ cup =
5⅓ tablespoons
2⅔ ounces

¼ cup =
4 tablespoons
2 ounces

3 teaspoons = 1 tablespoon (½ ounce)
2 tablespoons = ⅛ cup (1 ounce)
4 tablespoons = ¼ cup (2 ounces)
5⅓ tablespoons = ⅓ cup (2⅔ ounces)
8 tablespoons = ½ cup (4 ounces)
12 tablespoons = ¾ cup (6 ounces)
32 tablespoons = 2 cups (16 ounces)

Chapter 1

BATTER UP SNACK MIX

Jenna watched her brother walk up to home plate. She dug her hand into the bag of snack mix she had made.

"Mmm," she said. "This is sweet and salty. It's perfect to eat while watching the game!"

Crack! Luke hit the ball hard. It sailed over the fence. Home run!

Jenna cheered as Luke ran around the bases. He stopped and grabbed a handful of her snack. “Nice hit, Luke!” Jenna said, happy to share.

You will need:

8-ounce bag of kettle corn

8-ounce bag of small pretzels

8-ounce bag of chocolate candies

1 stick of butter

8-ounce box of cheese crackers

2 cups of rice or corn cereal

1 cup of peanuts

Directions:

Place the butter in a small bowl. Have an adult microwave the butter for 30–60 seconds or until it is melted.

Mix all the other ingredients together in a large bowl.

Pour the butter over the ingredients. Mix well with a large spoon.

Divide into smaller **portions**. Pack in plastic sandwich bags or serve in baseball-cap dishes.

FUN FOOD FACT!
Peanuts and popcorn have been popular snacks at baseball games for more than 100 years.

Chapter 2

COURTSIDE CHEESY CRUNCH DIP

Ben and Nick sat in front of the TV. Their favorite basketball team was about to play.

"Watching basketball always makes me hungry," Nick said. "Do you have any snacks?"

Ben’s mom walked into the room and set a big bowl in front of them. “I know what you mean,” she said. “Have some dip. I think you will like it.”

“Thanks!” Ben said happily. The game was sure to be even better with this tasty snack!

You will need:

8-ounce bag of **shredded** cheddar cheese

8-ounce tub of soft cream cheese

8-ounce tub of sour cream

8-ounce jar of salsa (Mild or spicy—it's up to you!)

2 green onions

16-ounce bag of tortilla chips

Directions:

Ask an adult to **chop** the onions into small pieces.

Mix the cream cheese and sour cream together.

Spread the mixture across the bottom of a 9-inch by 13-inch baking dish.

Pour the salsa on top of the cheese mixture.

Sprinkle the green onions over the salsa mixture.

Top with a layer of shredded cheese.

Serve with tortilla chips for dipping.

Chapter 3

TOUCHDOWN SLIDERS

Dennis and Terry hurried inside. They were cold and muddy. "We had a great game of football," Dennis told his mom. "But now we're hungry!"

"I'm glad you had fun," their mother said. "I knew you would want something to warm you up, so I made a winning snack for you football players. I know you will like these hot sliders."

She shook her head at their muddy clothes. "But first, please change your clothes and wash your hands!"

You will need:

12-ounce bag of frozen meatballs

1 bag of Hawaiian sweet rolls

8-ounce package of provolone cheese slices

8-ounce jar of pizza sauce or spaghetti sauce

Grated Parmesan cheese

Cooking spray

Directions:

Have an adult **thaw** the bag of meatballs in the microwave for 8–10 minutes.

Spray the bottom of the dish with cooking spray.

Cut each roll in half. Put them in the baking dish.

Place a slice of cheese on each half.

Top each half with a meatball.

Add a spoonful of sauce on top of each meatball.

Sprinkle Parmesan cheese over each meatball.

Place the other halves of the rolls on each slider.

Cover the dish with foil.

Ask an adult to bake the sliders in the oven at 350 degrees Fahrenheit (177 degrees Celsius) for 20 minutes.

FUN FOOD FACT!
Sliders got their name because they are small and greasy. They could slide right down your throat!

Chapter 4

FIELD DAY FRUIT BOWL

Kaylee ran off the soccer field. "Great job, Kaylee!" her mom called. "Come have a snack."

Kaylee grabbed some melon balls from the snack container. "These taste great!" she said. "Running around makes me so thirsty. These are cold and sweet. That is just what I needed."

Soon Kaylee was ready to get back to the game. She ran onto the field. She could not wait to play some more!

You will need:

1 watermelon

1 honeydew

1 **cantaloupe**

Directions:

Have an adult cut each melon in half. Scoop out any seeds inside.

Use a melon baller to scoop out melon balls from the honeydew and cantaloupe. Place them in a large bowl.

Move onto the watermelon. Once all the watermelon has been scooped out, scrape out any leftover bits with a spoon.

Now you can use the watermelon as a bowl for your melon balls!

FUN FOOD FACT!
A watermelon is approximately 92 percent water.

GLOSSARY

allergic (uh-LER-jik)—having a bad reaction to food

cantaloupe (KAN-tuh-lope)—a small melon with orange fruit

chop (CHOP)—cut into small pieces

grated (GRAY-ted)—rubbed into tiny pieces

portions (POR-shunz)—smaller parts of a meal

shredded (SHRED-ed)—torn into strips

sprinkle (SPRIN-kuhl)—drop small bits onto something

thaw (THAW)—to unfreeze

FURTHER READING

Kartes, Danielle. *My Very First Cookbook.* Sourcebooks Explore, 2020.

Nissenberg, Sandra K. *The Everything Kids' Cookbook.* Simon & Schuster, 2020.

ON THE INTERNET

"Five Easy Football Day Snacks to Make with Kids." Roanoke.MacaroniKid.com
https://roanoke.macaronikid.com/guides/6205f972568c3c2ca16f9346/five-easy-football-day-snacks-to-make-with-kids
From clever sandwiches to beautiful cupcakes, the article includes several fun football-themed recipes for kids and parents to make together.

"Kid-Approved Game Day Snack Ideas." Health.FMOLHS.org
https://health.fmolhs.org/body/eating-well/kid-approved-game-day-snack-ideas/
Kids and parents will find lots of great game day snack ideas in this article!

INDEX

ABOUT THE AUTHOR

Joanne Mattern loves snacking and eating fun food! She has written many nonfiction books for children, including cookbooks and books about holidays. Joanne lives in New York State with her family.